There was joy in writing this book. Joy in hearing Stuart's stories of those special moments with his grandmother. Joy in remembering the night stars I saw as a child with my naked eye in the stark darkness of Kisatchie National Forest where I grew up. Joy in hearing the Maker's words again. Much needed to hear...He knows my name.

—Cay

The stars, as well as the cosmos in its entirety (however far reaching that is), have always been a source of wonder and fascination for me. The awe I feel when looking up to behold the heavens has remained a cosmological constant. As above, so below!

—Stuart

Look Up, Sealy

Written by
Cay Evans, PhD

Illustrated by
Jaylin Monroe

SEALY

Look up, Sealy. Look up.

SEALY

In the blanket of dark night, the stars and other wonders of the universe shined brightly.

The magic of the night sky
appeared all around.

The stars with their glowing points.

The moon with it shadows.

The constellations with their figures.

God said to us that he counted the stars and he knows them by their names. All reminding us of how big God is.

SEALY

SEALY

And how much he loves us.

Look up, Sealy. Look up.

SEALY

God knows us by our names, too!

Roderick
Martha
Brielle
Joseph
Nicholas
Emily
John
Greyson
Cole
Steven
Maria
Richard
Pat
Clay
David
Rebecca
Pam
Mary
Joy
Jonah
Kate
Donald
Eloise
Allen
Peace
Madison
Beau
Miracle
Parker

SEACY

Look up, Sealy. Look up.

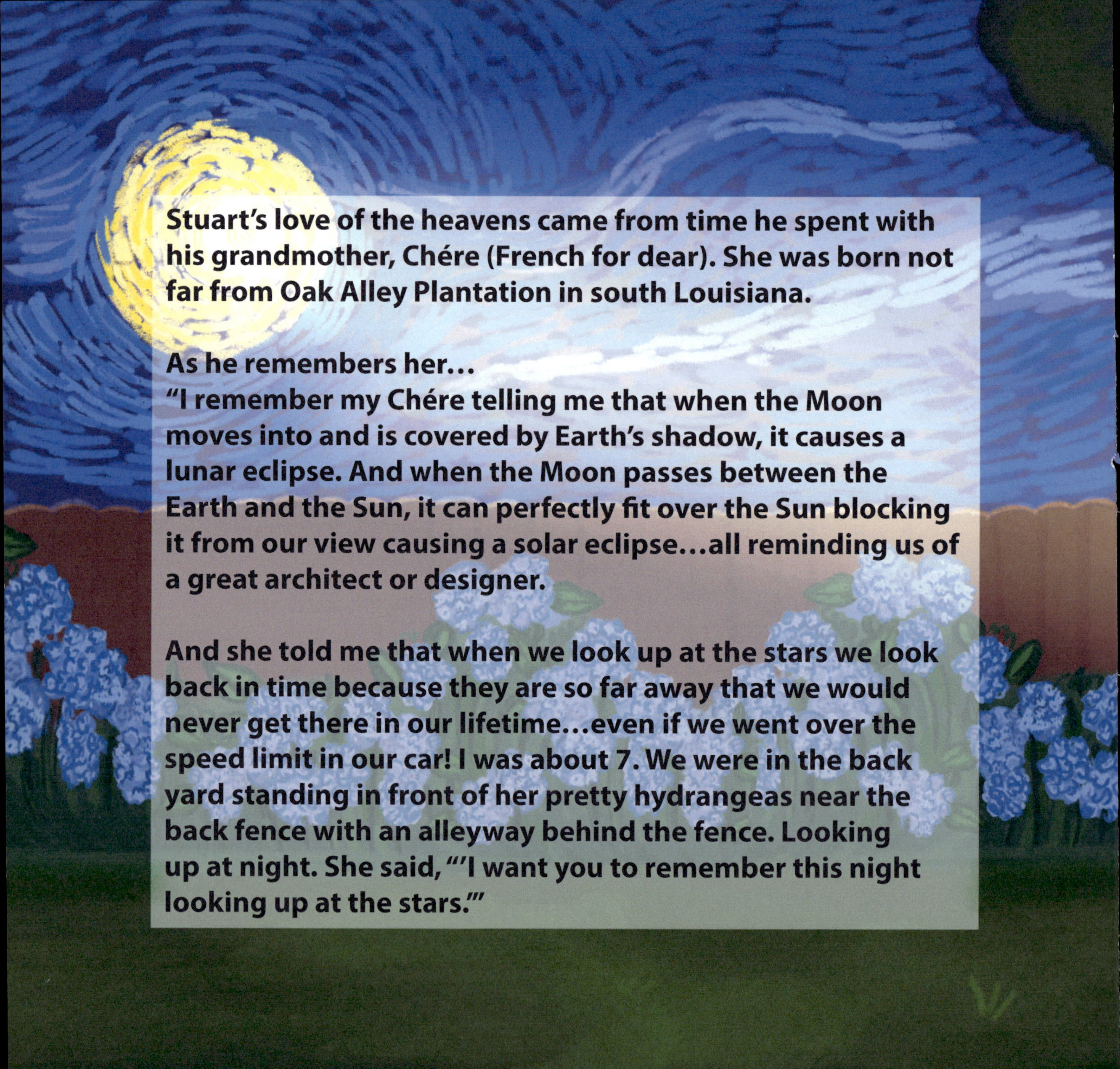

Stuart's love of the heavens came from time he spent with his grandmother, Chére (French for dear). She was born not far from Oak Alley Plantation in south Louisiana.

As he remembers her...
"I remember my Chére telling me that when the Moon moves into and is covered by Earth's shadow, it causes a lunar eclipse. And when the Moon passes between the Earth and the Sun, it can perfectly fit over the Sun blocking it from our view causing a solar eclipse...all reminding us of a great architect or designer.

And she told me that when we look up at the stars we look back in time because they are so far away that we would never get there in our lifetime...even if we went over the speed limit in our car! I was about 7. We were in the back yard standing in front of her pretty hydrangeas near the back fence with an alleyway behind the fence. Looking up at night. She said, "'I want you to remember this night looking up at the stars.'"

ISBN: 978-1-955755-33-7

Made in the USA
Columbia, SC
15 November 2024